THE
Archive Photographs
SERIES
MONTGOMERYSHIRE

Powis Castle, near Welshpool.

THE
Archive Photographs
SERIES
MONTGOMERYSHIRE

Compiled by
Eva Bredsdorff

CHALFORD

First published 1996
Copyright © Eva Bredsdorff, 1996

The Chalford Publishing Company
St Mary's Mill, Chalford,
Stroud, Gloucestershire, GL6 8NX

ISBN 0 7524 0378 8

Typesetting and origination by
The Chalford Publishing Company
Printed in Great Britain by
Redwood Books, Trowbridge

Contents

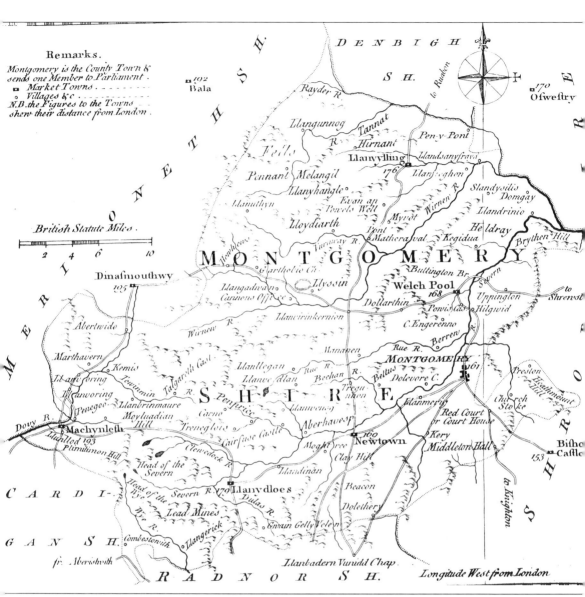

Map of Montgomeryshire dating from 1759. The old county of Montgomeryshire lies in mid-Wales. It is bordered by England to the east, by the River Dovey and the Welsh coast in the west, by the Berwyn Mountains and the River Tanat in the north and by Radnorshire and the valley of the River Severn in the south.

6

WELSHPOOL. BREIDDIN HILLS & RIVER SEVERN.

The River Severn near Welshpool with the Breidden Hills in the background.

Introduction

Montgomeryshire lies in Mid-Wales. The rivers Severn, Wye and Vyrnwy start here and they wind their way through a landscape of imposing mountains and hills and lush and beautiful lowland. In English the county is named after Roger de Montgomery. He was a Norman who came to England in the service of William the Conqueror, by whom he was made earl of Shrewsbury. In Welsh the county is called Sir Maldwyn and is named after Baldwin, a lieutenant to the same king.

Apart from the Ordovician dolerite of the Breidden Hills and Corndon Hill, the geology of Montgomeryshire consists of sedimentary rocks dating from the Ordovician and Silurian periods. During the Caledonian earth movements these strata were lifted up and strongly folded to create the hills and mountains of today. The Severn valley resulted from glaciation as the rock was slowly eroded away by the ice. The landscape is dominated by mountains and hills, many over 2000ft above sea level and most over 1000ft, by green grasslands and forests of oak and ash and by east flowing rivers, especially the Severn in its broad and fertile valley. In the sixth century the poet Llywarch Hen called the area 'Powys paradwys Cymru' - Powys, the paradise of Wales.

The earliest evidence of man is some Mesolithic stone implements. But it was not until the Neolithic period that people settled in the area, probably as early farmers. Signs of occupation has been found at Ffridd Faldwyn and the Breidden Hills. The so-called 'Beaker people', supposedly originating in Mid-Europe, came to the area around 2000 BC. They brought with them a distinctive style of pottery and a knowledge of metallurgy which was decisive in the change of material for tools and weapons from stone to copper and bronze. Evidence of the Beaker people has been found at Hyssington. Knowledge of life during the Bronze Age comes, paradoxically, mostly from the dead and their graves, especially those in round barrows, some of which can be seen at Caebetin Hill near Kerry and by Llanbrynmair. The Early Bronze Age agricultural economy was probably dominated by cattle rearing and hunting which seems to have brought wealth and prosperity.

Monuments such as stone and wooden circles and stone rows point towards a religion focusing on the worship of sun or sky gods. Most Bronze Age finds date to the Middle Bronze Age and consist mostly of hoards of bronze items such as axes, palstaves, swords and spears. The motive behind the burial of such possessions still puzzles the experts. Hoards have been found at Guilsfield, Buttington and other places in the county. During the Iron Age the area was dominated by hillforts. They may have been either military strongholds or social and economic centres controlling the surrounding area of farmland and grazing, or a combination of both.

During the first century AD the Romans began their occupation of Britain. The native population at the time consisted of tribes, some of which unsuccessfully tried to oppose the Romans. The most famous tribal ruler was Caratacus (the Caradog of Welsh tradition) whose last battle against the Romans is said to have taken place in Montgomeryshire in AD 51. Most communities in Montgomeryshire were absorbed into the Roman province. To maintain authority over the area the Romans built a network of forts and camps connected by roads. The main forts of Montgomeryshire were Caersws and Forden Gaer which were linked by a road probably running along the eastern bank of the River Severn. These forts remained occupied until Roman rule in Britain came to an end in the fifth century.

Very few archaeological finds have been made for the five hundred years following the Roman withdrawal and the most spectacular evidence remains Offa's Dyke, the earthwork which stretches from Prestatyn in the north to the Severn estuary in the south. It defined the frontier between Mercia and Wales from the late eighth century. It bears the name of the Mercian king, Offa who ruled from 757 to 796 and may have been a defensive barrier or more probably, an agreed-to border demarcation.

During the Middle Ages the history of Montgomeryshire was intertwined with that of the princes of Powys Wenwynwyn and thus the county often became the battleground for clashes between the Welsh and the English. These included the raids by Llywelyn ap Gruffudd in the thirteenth century, the conflict between (the later) Edward III and Queen Isabella in the 1320s and the last great rebellion of the Welsh under Owain Glyn Dŵr in the fifteenth century. The Act of Union in 1536 during the reign of Henry VIII united England and Wales and created twelve counties one of which was Montgomeryshire. Through the centuries the main occupation of the area has been sheep and cattle farming and today the county has only a few towns with the biggest, Newtown, having no more than 10,000 inhabitants. During the nineteenth century the county did see an increase in its flannel and woollen industry and the area became one of the most important producers and exporters of wool in Great Britain. However, the industry was strangled by competition both from England and overseas during the first decade of the twentieth century.

Today Montgomeryshire forms part of the Powys Unitary Authority together with Radnorshire and Breconshire. It is still a tranquil county, with a strong farming community and some minor industries, and has increasingly become a popular destination for visitors both from the rest of the British Isles and from abroad.

This volume on Montgomeryshire for the Archive Photographs Series has been compiled from material in the collection at Powysland Museum in Welshpool. It is not, therefore, a complete record of all the towns and villages in the area but rather an impression of the county based on the available images in the museum collection. The museum still actively collects memorabilia from Montgomeryshire and would be grateful for more photographs especially of places not represented in the book.

One
Welshpool

General view of Welshpool from Red Bank, *c.* 1960. This market town lies four miles from the border between Wales and England and is the gateway to mid-Wales. It is a charming town with several attractions for the whole family.

Broad Street in the 1920s. This is the main street and part of the medieval layout of Welshpool. Today it is the commercial centre of the town.

A bustling Broad Street, c. 1930. Although many of the shop fronts have been modernized, most of the houses are still recognizable today.

Broad Street, viewed from the balcony of the Town Hall, probably in the 1950s.

A rare view of High Street, *c.* 1900, taken from the top of the town and looking towards the Town Hall and Broad Street.

High Street, Welshpool looking towards Mount Street and the top of the town, *c.* 1960. The Methodist church on the left hand side was built by George Bidlake in 1863. The black and white building is one of the earliest houses in the town, dating back to the seventeenth century.

High Street, Welshpool, from the balcony of the Town Hall, 1950s. The Pheasant Inn on the right hand side is still open today.

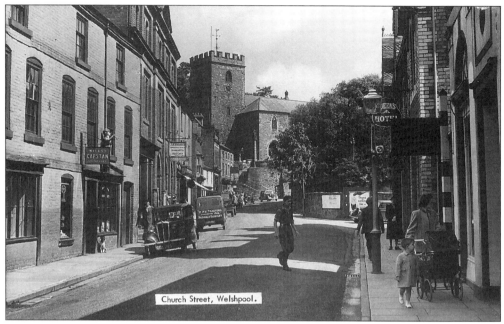

Church Street, Welshpool.

Church Street, Welshpool, *c*. 1960. This photograph covers the view of the street towards St Mary's Church and includes the Queen's Hotel and J.M. Morris, ironmongers.

Church Street, Welshpool, *c*. 1960, photographed from outside St Mary's Church and looking towards The Cross - the centre of town where Church Street meets Broad Street, Severn Street and Berriew Street.

Berriew Street, *c.* 1960, looking towards The Cross. The Angel public house on the left is still serving drinks, while the Pola Cinema, advertising on the right hand side, is still showing movies. It is situated just outside the picture to the right.

Severn Street, *c.* 1960. Most of the houses here are Georgian buildings dating from the nineteenth century. The street crosses the Montgomery Canal and leads down to the railway station.

Union Street with St Mary's Church, 1920s.

The Smithfield market, 1960s. The largest weekly one-day sheep market in Europe is held here every Monday thus transforming Welshpool from a quiet, relaxed town to the bustling, busy centre for farmers from near and far.

The Town Hall in Welshpool. This was built by Benjamin Lay in 1873-74, although the façade was later changed to its present-day appearance in 1881.

The backroad from Welshpool towards Llanfair Caereinion, *c*. 1930. A last look at the town including Christ Church and part of Powis Park.

Two
Newtown

Newtown in 1846. In January 1279 Edward I granted a charter to Roger Mortimer authorising the establishment of a market every Tuesday and two fairs each year in the little hamlet of Llanfair yng Nghedewain (St Mary's Church in Cedewain). A town was laid out with a central thoroughfare - today's Broad Street and High Street. By the early fourteenth century it was known as Newtown.

Broad Street, *c.* 1960.

The Cross and Broad Street. The Midland Bank building on the corner stands on the site of the birthplace of Robert Owen (1771-1858). He has been called the father of British socialism and was the pioneer of the co-operative movement, spokesman for factory reforms and founder of nursery schools, mostly in Lancashire. At the age of ten he was apprenticed to a draper in Stamford and after working in London he borrowed money to establish his own workshop in Manchester. In 1800 he went to New Lanark in Scotland where he purchased a mill and set about improving conditions. His new factory worked on model lines, refusing to employ young children, giving older ones further education, limiting working hours for adults and establishing a co-operative store. In the last year of his long and prolific life, Owen returned to Newtown where he died and was buried.

Fair Day, Broad Street, *c.* 1880. The market has existed for seven hundred years and is held every Tuesday. The first market hall dates from *c.* 1570, while a later building was erected in 1769 and pulled down in 1852. Today the market takes place on the street.

High Street, Newtown. This photograph was taken before the building of Barclay's Bank. The black and white building on the left is the Buck Inn which dates back to the seventeenth century.

High Street, Newtown. The postcard is postmarked 1906 and the picture includes Barclay's Bank.

High Street, Newtown showing its typical nineteenth century shop-fronts.

High Street, c. 1960. This shows the street from The Cross looking towards the grounds of the old Newtown Hall, today the new Town Hall. The photograph was taken on market day.

Fair Day in Newtown's High Street, *c*. 1880.

The north side of Severn Street, postmarked 1915. The houses in this area of the town date from the eighteenth century.

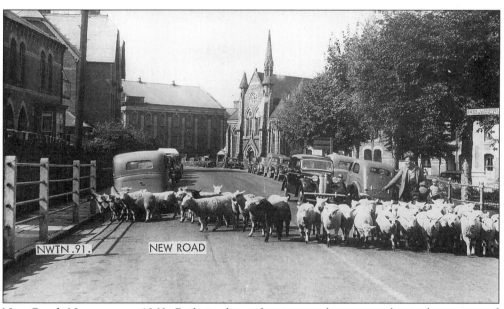

New Road, Newtown, c. 1960. Built in the early nineteenth century, this is the main road through Newtown going towards Welshpool, Llandrindod Wells, Llanidloes and Dolgellau. In the background are the Zion Baptist Tabernacle (to the left) built in 1881 by George Morgan, and the Welsh Calvinistic Methodist Church (to the right) built between 1875 and 1876.

Town Clock at The Cross in Newtown, *c*. 1950. Barclay's Bank, with its imposing clock tower, was built in 1898 by Wood and Kendrick of Birmingham to celebrate the Diamond Jubilee of Queen Victoria.

The Town Hall, *c*. 1960. The building stands on the site of Newtown Hall. It was built between 1965 and 1968 by Colwyn Foulkes & Partners. It houses county chambers and offices.

The Royal Welsh Warehouse. In 1861 local businessman Sir Pryce Pryce-Jones started the first ever mail order company. His business expanded to include steam woollen mills and a laundry. In the 1870s he opened the Royal Welsh Warehouse as an early department store. The architect was David Walker of Liverpool.

View of Newtown. From around 1790 Newtown became known as 'the Leeds of Wales' due to its woollen production. At first, handlooms dominated the town but after a period of stagnation during the middle of the nineteenth century, the industry was revived, powerlooms were installed and Welsh flannel was produced for an ever increasing market. However, by the end of the nineteenth century competition from other British and foreign woollen industries decimated the production of flannel in Newtown and the last major mill was closed in 1935.

Three

Other major Montgomeryshire towns

Machynlleth, a town in the western part of Montgomeryshire, standing at the head of the estuary of the River Dovey. The town's charter was granted by Edward I to Owain de la Pole, prince of Powys in 1291.

General view of Machynlleth. The town's history is dominated by the fifteenth century heroic figure of Owain Glyn Dŵr . He was both a descendant of the princes of Powys and related to the Tudors. He was a poet, a lawyer and a general in the English army, acquiring the title of Sir Owen Knight of the Glen. However, he led a Welsh rebellion against the English and obtained a fleeting independence for Wales.

General view of Machynlleth. Due to the geography of the area the medieval town plan is T-shaped. From 1798 there was a coach link with England and the railway reached the town in 1864.

The Clock Tower in Maengwyn Street, Machynlleth, *c*. 1960. The Clock Tower was erected in 1873 to mark the coming of age of Lord Castlereagh, the eldest son of the Marquis of Londonderry who lived at Plas Machynlleth. It was designed by Henry Kennedy.

The Old Market Hall in Llanidloes. An old market town in south Montgomeryshire, the town was granted a market charter in 1280 by King Edward I. The sixteenth century timber-framed market hall is the oldest surviving in Wales. The upper room was used for the assizes while a large stone at the north west corner is said to have been used as a platform by John Wesley when he was preaching in the town.

The Old Market Hall, Llanidloes.

Longbridge Street, Llanidloes. The town has always been very active both in religious and political matters and it has several non-conformist chapels. The first Sunday school in Wales is said to have been held in the town in 1770.

The corner of Great Oak Street and China Street, Llanidloes, 1950s. During the nineteenth century the town had a large weaving industry and it was amongst the weavers that social dissatisfaction could be found. Llanidloes became one of the Welsh centres for the Chartist movement. In 1839 the first violence associated with Chartism in Wales took place in Llanidloes. On 20 April three London policemen were despatched to the town at the request of the local magistrates. On the following day these officers were attacked in the Trewythen Hotel and the men they had arrested freed. The hotel was subsequently looted and a week passed before the magistrates intervened again. During this period Llanidloes was effectly controlled by local Chartists. Debate still exists as to whether the disturbances were instigated by Chartist rebels or were 'provoked' by the authorities to 'smoke out' political opponents. The result was that three men were transported to Australia.

Llanfyllin, c. 1905. A market town lying north-west of Welshpool, it was granted its charter by Llywelyn ap Gruffydd ap Gwenwynwyn, Lord Mechain in 1293.

Lonely tree and Allthygyda Hill at Llanfyllin, c. 1914. The town is situated in a very beautiful area. The lonely tree stands not far from St Myllin's Well, which was also named after the saint. Sick visitors used to tie rags to bushes near the well in the belief that by so doing they would recover their health.

General view of Llanfyllin, *c*. 1960.

The Square in Llanfyllin, *c*. 1960. At the top of Market Street is The Hall, where Charles I stayed as the guest of Sir John Price when he was on his way to Chirk during the Civil War.

Montgomery, the Market Place. This is the old county town of Montgomeryshire and was named after Roger de Montgomery, 1st earl of Shrewsbury, who was a Norman in the service of William the Conqueror. The town received its first charter in 1227.

Broad Street and the Town Hall, Montgomery, c. 1960. The town has an almost unchanged medieval town plan with well preserved Georgian buildings and cobble-stoned pavements. The Town Hall was built by William Baker in 1748. The clock tower was added in 1921.

Memorial gardens and chapel, Montgomery, *c.* 1960.

The new estate in Montgomery, *c.* 1950

The Lower town, Montgomery, c. 1960.

Main road, Montgomery. The town was originally walled with four gates called Arthur, Cedewain, Chirbury and Ceri. Parts of the wall can still be seen.

View of Llanymynech from the River Bridge, *c.* 1960. The town lies on the Welsh-English border, north of Welshpool, in the shadow of the 900 ft Llanymynech hill. On the top of this hill is a popular golf course where you can drive a ball from a tee in Wales to a green in England.

The main street in Llanymynech, 1950s. The Romans were very active in the area and many contemporary archaeological items have been found. It is said that the area was the scene of the last stand of Caratacus in AD 51. He was one of the British tribal leaders who organised resistance against the Roman army of occupation until he was finally defeated and captured.

The main street in Llanymynech, 1950s. During the centuries the town has been the centre of limestone quarrying. It also had a busy railway line and there was much traffic on the nearby Montgomery Canal. Today, it is a more tranquil place.

Penyfoel, near Llanymynech, c. 1908. The photograph is taken from Pant Road.

General View, Llanfair Caereinion.

The market town of Llanfair Caereinion west of Welshpool, *c.* 1938. The town developed during the eighteenth and nineteenth centuries and once had thriving flannel and tanning industries.

View from High Street, Llanfair Caereinion, *c.* 1905. Samuel Roberts was a famous local clockmaker, who worked in the town at the end of the eighteenth century. There is a sundial made by him in the town's churchyard and one of his clocks can be seen in Powysland Museum in nearby Welshpool.

General view of Llanfair Caereinion, *c.* 1960. Today the town is mostly famous for the Welshpool-Llanfair Caereinion Light Railway. After years of discussions the railway was built in 1903 and it ran between the two towns until 1956. Since the 1960s a preservation society has worked to conserve and run the railway for the benefit of visitors to the area.

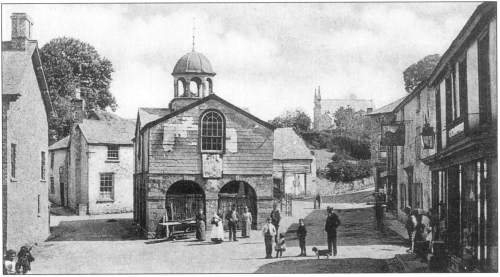

Old Market Hall, Llanfair Caereinion. This market hall was built in the late eighteenth century and contained a schoolroom. It was demolished around 1890 before which this photograph must have been taken.

Four
Villages in Montgomeryshire

Bettws Cedewain, looking north, c. 1905. This is a small village between Newtown and Welshpool. Built around the crossings over the river Bechan, it contains some beautiful black and white buildings dating from the seventeenth century.

The main street of Caersws, a large village between Newtown and Llanidloes, *c.* 1960. It was the site, at the crossing of five roads, of an important Roman fort. In English the name means 'defended place of Sws' with 'Sws' refering to an otherwise unidentified person.

Llys Maldwyn in Caersws, *c.* 1960. Formerly the workhouse for the Poor Law Union of Newtown and Llanidloes, it was built in 1840. Today the building is a hospital.

General view of Carno, a village north-west of Caersws, from the river, *c.* 1960. According to one legend the name of Carno stems from a hill in the centre of the parish called Clorin, the shape of which resembles a horse. The word clorin dated from Roman times and means horse while 'carn' in Welsh can mean 'hoof'. Other sources suggest that the village is named after the surrounding cairns or the river Cerniog. The village is the site of the original Laura Ashley factory, first started in 1963. Laura Ashley died in 1985 and she is buried in Carno.

Aleppo Merchant Hotel in Carno, *c.* 1960. It was formerly the Ty Ucha, but was renamed after his ship by a sea captain who became its landlord.

General view of Castle Caereinion a small village near Welshpool, *c.* 1960. It is said that Henry Tudor (later Henry VII) rested at Dolarddyn Hall, just outside the village, on the 13 August 1485 on his way to fight Richard III at the battle of Bosworth Field. The hall has since been demolished.

The rectory attached to St Garmon's Church, Castle Caereinion, *c.* 1880. The church dates from the nineteenth century although the churchyard contains a mound which may be the site of an old motte and bailey castle from which the village derives its name.

General view of Churchstoke a large village on the Montgomeryshire-Shropshire border, *c*. 1960. Excavations near the town have revealed Simon's Castle, the foundations of a small Norman castle built on a natural rock outcrop like a motte.

The bridge at Churchstoke, *c*. 1960, with the crossroads to Welshpool and Newtown.

Churchstoke bridge, *c.* 1950.

The village of Dolanog, north-west of Welshpool. The name like the vast majority in Montgomeryshire derives from Welsh and means either 'woolly meadow' or a meadow used for a gathering. The local church of St John was built in the nineteenth century.

Dolwar Fach. Dolanog is especially associated with the hymn writer, Ann Griffiths. She was born at Dolwar Fach in 1776 and died young in 1805. She was buried at nearby Llanfihangel-yng-Ngwynfa with her two-week old baby. The Ann Griffiths Memorial Chapel was built in 1903.

Plas Dolanog, a partly timber-framed building dating from 1664. It was the home of the Williams-Wynn family.

Llan, *c.* 1905. This village was originally called Llanbrynmair but by the end of the nineteenth century this name had passed to the cluster of houses situated around the Wynnstay Arms, over a mile to the north of the old village which was then renamed 'Llan'. The famous reformer and preacher Samuel Roberts was born in the village in 1800.

Llandyssil, a small village between Welshpool and Newtown, *c.* 1905. The old church of St Tyssil once stood higher on the hillside. It was pulled down in 1865 and now only a fifteenth century stone porch remains in the churchyard.

The main street in Llandyssil, *c*. 1960.

A second view of the main street in Llandyssil, *c*. 1960.

The village of Llanerfyl, west of Llanfair Caereinion. The origins of the village church of St Erfyl are ancient and it contains one of the earliest Christian gravestones in Wales dating from the late fifth or early sixth century. There is a small twelfth century motte and bailey castle nearby.

Llanerfyl village, 1950s.

Llangynog village, north-west of Llanfyllin, *c.* 1905. During the eighteenth and nineteenth centuries the area of the village was an important centre for lead mining and also slate and granite quarrying. The site, however, had already been in use in the early medieval era. The church of St Cynog dates from the late eighteenth and the nineteenth century.

Llanrhaedr-ym-Mochnant, a small village on the border between the old counties of Montgomeryshire and Denbighshire, c. 1905. Four miles from the village is the famous waterfall of Pistyll Rhaeadr, considered one of the most spectacular sights in Wales.

The old market hall at Llanrhaedr-ym-Mochant, 1890s. Long since demolished, this was similar to the one in Llanidloes.

Broad Street in the village of Meifod. The princes of Powys are said to have held their courts near here in the eighth century.

Keel bridge in Meifod. A twelfth century poet, Cynddelw wrote:

Who hath seen the territory fair
Of Smiling Meifod, shall not see the like
Nor tho' his life till Doomsday be prolonged.

The Breidden Hotel in the small village of Middletown on the Wales-England border, northeast of Welshpool, 1950s.

Old Parr's Cottage in Middletown. This was supposedly once the home of William Parr, a local man who is said to have been born in 1483, to have married at the age of 80, and again, after his first wife's death, at the age of 122. His fame reached the court of Charles I and in 1635 he went to London to see the king. He died the same year at the ripe age of 152 years and was buried in Westminster Abbey. He thus allegedly lived during the reigns of ten monarchs: Edward IV, Edward V, Richard III, Henry VII, Henry VII, Edward VI, Mary Tudor, Elizabeth I, James I and Charles I.

The Breidden Hills, on the border between Wales and England. On one of the hills a pillar was erected in 1781 by the people of Montgomeryshire in honour of Admiral Sir George Brydges Rodney. He was celebrated because he had insisted on using Montgomeryshire oak when building ships for the Navy, thus supporting the local economy.

New houses at Penegoes, a small village close to Machynlleth. The village is first recorded in 1254 and the name probable means 'head (or upper part) of the ridge or spur of land'.

Tainewyddion at Penegoes. The village is the birthplace of the famous Welsh landscape painter Richard Wilson who lived from 1714 to 1782. He was born in the old rectory, which has since been demolished.

The mill at Penegoes. This seventeenth century water mill on the river Crewi has been restored and is still in use today.

Station Road in Penybontfawr, c. 1950.

General view of Penybontfawr, a village situated in a predominantly Welsh-speaking area north-west of Llanfyllin, 1950s. Most of the houses date from the nineteenth century.

The village of Penybontfawr, 1950s. The harpist, Nansi Richards, was born in the village in 1888. At the age of 20 she won the triple harp competition at Llangollen National Eisteddfod. A scholarship in her honour is awarded to a talented young harpist every year.

Penybontfawr, 1950s.

The bridge at Penybontfawr, c. 1905. *Er pob newid a fu, neu a fydd yn y dyfodol, hyderwn y deil yr iaith Gymraeg yn ein bro, mor gadarn a'r hen bont a roddodd enw i'n pentref.* Despite past and future changes, we trust that the Welsh language in our area will remain as firm as the bridge that gave the village its name.

The village of Pontrobert between Llanfair Caereinion and Llanfyllin, looking east, 1930s. It is named after Robert ap Oliver of Cynhinfa. He had the bridge over the river rebuilt after it had been swept away by floods in 1633.

The Royal Oak at Pontrobert, 1950s.

Pontrobert, looking north. The nearby Dolobran Hall has been the family home of the Lloyd family since 1425. One of the family members was Samson Lloyd, the founder of Lloyd's Bank.

The post office in Staylittle, a village by the Llyn Clywedog Reservoir, not far from Llanidloes, 1950s. The English name comes from a legend about two local blacksmith brothers who could shoe horses so quickly that their customers only had to 'stay a little'. The Welsh name of Penfforddlas means 'common at the top of the green road'.

The village of Trewern, north of Welshpool, c. 1960. The name means 'township of the alders or swamp' in Welsh. The village lies at the foot of the Breidden Hills, the nearest of which is the 1,324ft high Moel y Golfa, meaning 'bald or stony hill'. The school and community centre were built in 1953.

Five
Water

Bridge over the river Vyrnwy at Pont Robert.

The two bridges over the River Severn at Buttington, near Welshpool, *c.* 1880.

On the River Severn at Welshpool, *c.* 1880. In the medieval period the town was known as 'Pola' from the several small pools in the area. The name was changed to Welch or Welshpool in the sixteenth century to distinguish it from Poole in Dorest. The spelling varied between 'Welch' and 'Welsh' pool until the late nineteenth century when Welshpool prevailed.

The River Rhiw at Berriew, near Welshpool, *c*. 1925. The name of the village comes from the Welsh 'Aberriw' - 'the mouth of the River Rhiw'. The anglicised form of today dates back to the middle of the eighteenth century.

Canoeing on the River Severn at Llandyssil, *c*. 1960.

Long Bridge over the River Severn at Newtown, *c*. 1900. The bridge was built by William Pugh in order to improve communications between Newtown and the parish of Llanllwchaiarn on the other side of the river.

The River Severn viewed from Long Bridge showing the Old Church, c. 1900. Over the centuries Newtown has suffered from severe flooding but as a result of intensive preventative work carried out mainly in the 1960s and 1970s this problem has been eliminated.

Bridge over the Severn at Caersws, *c*. 1905. The bridge was built around 1821 and the flooding of past times has been prevented by the building of the Clywedog Dam.

The Severn Valley from Maes Hafren by Caersws, *c*. 1960.

Bridge over the River Severn at Llanidloes, *c.* 1960.

Bridge over the River Dovey north of Machynlleth.

A closer look at the bridge over the Dovey.

The Ffryd Bridge by Machynlleth, *c*. 1900.

Dulas Stream, Machynlleth.

Einion Valley, Machynlleth.

The weir on the River Tanat by Llanymynech, *c.* 1960. The village of Llanymynech lies between the two rivers, the Vyrnwy and the Tanat.

The Llanymynech bridge over the river Vyrnwy, *c.* 1960. The bridge was designed by Thomas Penson in 1826.

The River Vyrnwy south of Llanymynech, *c*. 1905.

Lake Vyrnwy and Dam, *c*. 1905. Work on the lake and dam started in July 1881 when the 3rd Earl of Powis laid the first commemorative stone. The engineers were Thomas Hawksley and George Frederick Deacon.

Lake Vyrnwy, 1914. This was the first masonry dam to be built in Great Britain. It is 84ft high and holds back 13 million gallons of water. Over a thousand men were employed in the project, of whom 44 died during construction. The total cost was more than £2 million.

Lake Vyrnwy Dam, 1950s. The lake was first filled in 1888 and it supplies water via Oswestry and Tarporley to Liverpool seventy miles away.

The dam and hotel, Lake Vyrnwy, *c*. 1908. The hotel was built in 1890 and offers a spectacular view of the dam and the lake.

Lake Vyrnwy, *c*. 1905. The old village of Llanwddyn, situated in the upper Vyrnwy valley, was 'drowned' to make way for the lake. This village consisted of a church, two chapels, three inns and 47 dwellings. The inhabitants of the 'drowned' village were rehoused by the Liverpool Corporation who were responsible for the construction of the dam and the lake. The new village, downstream from the reservoir, is now a thriving community.

THE STRAINING TOWER · LAKE VYRNWY

The straining tower of Lake Vyrnwy, *c*. 1925. This pump house was built by George Frederick Deacon who disguised its use by designing it as a stone fortress protected by a bridge, thus giving it a somewhat Germanic look. The tower still contains its original machinery.

Evening at Lake Vyrnwy, 1930s.

Clywedog Reservoir near Staylittle, *c.* 1960. The dam was built between 1964 and 1968 by Sir William Halcrow & Partners.

Clywedog Dam and Reservoir near Staylittle, *c.* 1960. The project was designed as a river-regulating reservoir, holding back the winter rains, to alleviate flooding of the River Severn.

Clywedog Dam near Staylittle, *c.* 1960. The 237ft high dam is the tallest mass of concrete in Great Britain. A recent Rover advertisement featured a car being driven up the concrete buttress of the dam.

The Montgomery Canal near Welshpool, 1920s. The first part of the canal, from Porthywaen to Welshpool and Garthmyl, was built between 1794 and 1797. The second and final part to Newtown was finished in 1821. In 1987 the British Waterways Board started restoration work after years of neglect and it is hoped that most of the canal will be totally restored and linked up with the English canal system by the millennium.

Six
Religious buildings in Towns

St Mary's Church near Welshpool. The church may be the 'Ecclesia de Pola' mentioned in the Norwich taxation of 1254. Although probably originally dedicated to St Cynfelyn, in the middle of the thirteenth century it was rededicated to St Mary of the Salutation.

St Mary's Church, Welshpool. The church has had several famous ministers. Among these was William Morgan, the translator of the Bible into Welsh, who resided here from 1575 to 1578.

Christ Church, Welshpool. The foundation stone of this church was laid by the Hon. Edward James Herbert, Viscount Clive, on Tuesday, 5 November 1839, the day on which he attained his majority. It was consecrated for divine worship on 2 October 1844.

Christ Church, Welshpool. The church was designed by Thomas Penson and is of the Anglo-Norman style of the nineteenth century. It is built in local Welshpool granite.

The old St Mary's Church in Newtown, 1958. The photograph is taken from across the River Severn.

The old St Mary's Church in Newtown, *c.* 1905. The church probably dates back to the thirteenth century. It was abandoned in the middle of the 1840s due to flooding. Today only the tower, restored in 1939, remains; the rest of the building is ruined.

The old St Mary's Church, Newtown, *c.* 1960. Here, there is a monument dedicated to Robert Owen. It was made by Alfred Toft in 1902 and consists of a portrait relief and a relief of labourers receiving justice at Robert Owen's hands.

St David's Church, Newtown. The church was built by Thomas Penson who also built Christ Church in Welshpool. On this occasion he decided to use a neo-Gothic design. It was finished in 1847.

All Saints' Church in Newtown, c. 1905. The church is built of limestone from Llanymynech. The architect was Aston Webb who built it for Sir Pryce Pryce-Jones between 1888 and 1890.

Church of God the Holy Ghost, Newtown, 1950s. This local Roman Catholic church developed in 1947 in a disused nineteenth century woollen factory.

St Peter's Church, Machynlleth, *c*. 1905. Although the original structure probably dates back to the thirteenth century, most of the church was rebuilt in 1827 by Edward Haycock Senior.

Christ Church, Machynlleth, *c*. 1905. This church was built by Henry Kennedy in 1881 but was later demolished.

St Idloes' Church, Llanidloes. The site of the church was chosen by the saint, Idloes, to whom the church is dedicated, in the seventh century. The tower dates from the fourteenth century, the arcade comes from the thirteenth century Cwmhir Abbey in Radnorshire and the roof was built during the reconstruction of the church in 1542.

St Myllin's Church, Llanfyllin. This parish church is dedicated to St Myllin, a sixth century Celtic saint. In the churchyard is the tomb of a great-grandfather and his great-grandson. The great-grandfather was rector in Llanfyllin during the Napoleonic Wars. His daughter fell in love with one of the French prisoners of war billeted in the town. To break up this relationship the rector made sure that the Frenchman was sent back to France, but following the rector's death, the Frenchman returned, married the rector's daughter and they both went to France to live. Years later their grandson returned to Llanfyllin and when he died, he was buried with his great-grandfather thus finally reconciling the family differences.

St Nicholas' Church, Montgomery. The church was founded around 1225 but many alterations have taken place since, especially in the nineteenth century. There are several monuments inside the church relating to the Herbert family of Chirbury.

St Nicholas' Church, Montgomery. In the graveyard is the 'Robber's Grave'. In 1821 John Davies was convicted of sheep stealing and hanged. He proclaimed his innocence and declared that no grass would grow over his grave for one hundred years; according to local tradition his words came true.

St Nicholas' Church, Montgomery, *c*. 1880.

St Agatha's Church, Llanymynech, c. 1950. The village lies on the border between Wales and England and the church is actually in Shropshire. It was rebuilt in 1843 in neo-Norman style. The clock, with its long pendulum, was designed and built by a local inventor, Richard Roberts.

St Mary's Church, Llanfair Caereinion, c. 1905. In 1239 the church was granted to the Cistercian nunnery at Llanllugan by the Bishop of St Asaph. However, although the building may incorporate details from the thirteenth century church, it is first and foremost the work of Edward Haycock Junior who supervised its rebuilding in 1868.

Seven

Religious Houses
in Villages

St Gwynnog's Church, Aberhafesp, *c.* 1905. There has been a church on the site since the twelfth century, but most of the present church dates from rebuilding in 1857. The name Aberhafesp means 'the mouth of the summer dry brook' in Welsh; 'aber' means 'mouth of the river', 'haf' is 'summer' and 'hesb' signifies 'dried up' or 'barren'.

St Beuno's Church and schoolhouse, Bettws-Cedewain. Founded in the sixth century, the church has probably the only pre-Reformation memorial brass in the county. This is dedicated to the memory of the Revd John ap Meredyth who died in 1531.

All Saints' Church, Buttington. The church's font reputedly comes from the now demolished Cistercian Abbey of Strata Marcella which was situated north of the church. Founded by Owain Cyfeiliog in 1170, the monastery was the largest in Wales. Following the 1536 order by Henry VIII for the dissolution of the monasteries, Lord Powis bought the buildings and removed all valuable items. Later the site was dismantled completely and the stonework sold off to other building sites in the area.

St Mary's Church, Caersws, *c*. 1905. This is a nineteenth century single-chamber church.

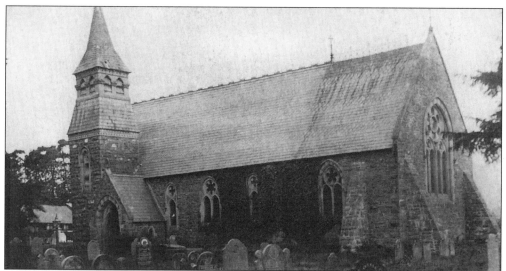
St John the Baptist's Church, Carno, *c*. 1905. There was an earlier medieval church belonging to the Knights of St John on the site. The present building was designed by the county surveyor, J.W. Poundley in 1863.

St Nicholas' Church, Churchstoke, *c.* 1905. The church has the oldest parish registers in Montgomeryshire dating from 1558. The Norman tower is the earliest part of the church but most of the building was either added or rebuilt in the nineteenth century.

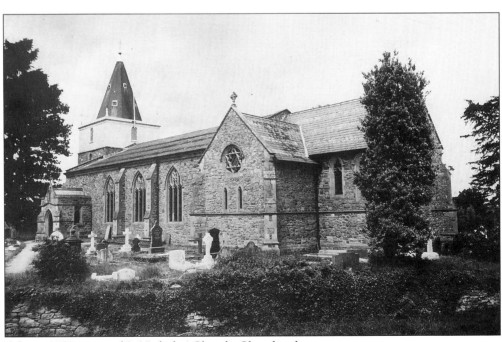

A later, 1950s, view of St Nicholas' Church, Churchstoke.

St Michael's Church, Forden, *c.* 1905. The church was designed and built by Thomas Nicholson; the foundation stone was laid on 19 June 1865 and the building was consecrated in 1867. The stained glass windows were made by William Morris & Co. from cartoons by the pre-Raphaelite artist, Sir Edward Burne-Jones.

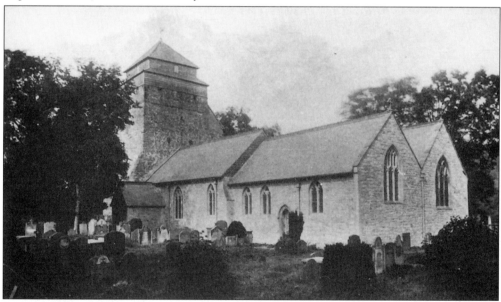

St Michael and All Angels' Church, Kerry, *c.* 1905. The church seems to have had a tumultuous early history. In 1176 its re-dedication resulted in a contest between the Bishop of St Asaph and Giraldus Cambrensis of St David's (Gerald of Wales). They both claimed the church and parish for their own diocese. They excommunicated each other, but Giraldus won the battle and the bishop had to flee the town under a bombardment of sticks and stones from the local people. The church was peacefully transferred to the diocese of St Asaph in 1849.

St Mary's Church, Llan, *c.* 1905. An earlier church on the site was founded in the seventh century by St Cadfan. Most of the present church dates from the fourteenth and fifteenth centuries.

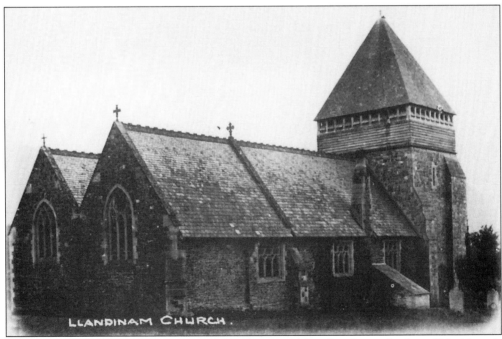

St Llonio's Church, Llandinam, *c.* 1905. The history of the church goes back to 520 although the present building was greatly restored in 1864-65 by G.E. Street. The old font has some deep incisions which are said to have been made by Oliver Cromwell's soldiers.

St Trinio, St Peter and St Paul's Church, Llandrinio, c. 1905. The history of this church goes back to the sixth century when it was dedicated to St Trinio. In the fourteenth century Edward II granted a concession to the village allowing it a three day fair annually on the festivals of St Peter and St Paul. Consequently, the church was renamed.

St Tyssil's Church, Llandyssil, c. 1905. The foundation stone for the new church was laid in 1863. Built to the designs of T.H. Wyatt, it was completed in 1866.

St Garmon's Church, Llanfechain, *c.* 1905. This is one of the most complete Norman churches in Montgomeryshire. The parish register dates back to 1597.

St Dogfan's Church, Llanrhaedr-ym-Mochnant, *c.* 1905. William Morgan was vicar of the parish for a period in the late sixteenth century; in 1588 he completed the first translation of the Bible into Welsh.

St Bride's Church, Llansantffraid-ym-Mechain, *c.* 1905. According to local legend the siting of the church was chosen by God. The inhabitants of the village wanted to build the church on the highest hill, Foel Hill, but whenever they had dragged the building stones to the summit, they would find them on the top of another hill when they returned the next day. In the end they decided that God wished for the church to be built there.

St Gwynnog's Church, Llanwnog, *c.* 1960. This is a single-chamber church. The walls incorporate medieval stonework and red sandstones from the Roman fort at Caersws. The church was heavily restored in 1863 and in 1982.

St Michael's Church, Manafon, *c.* 1905. The original church may date from the 1300s. During the nineteenth century it was twice substantially restored.

St Mary and St Tysilio's Church, Meifod. The first church of the village was founded in 550 by the missionary, Gwyddfach. In 728 a second church was dedicated to St Tysilio who was the son of a prince of Powys. Finally, in 1170, Prince Madog devoted a new church to St Mary. As with most of the churches in Montgomeryshire there are building details dating from the fourteenth and following centuries up to major restoration work taking place in the nineteenth century.

St Cadfarch's Church, Penegoes. The medieval church here was replaced by that pictured above which was designed by John Prichard in 1877.

St Thomas' Church, Pen-y-bont-fawr, c. 1900. This was built in 1855 by R.K. Penson.

St John Evangelist's Church, Pontrobert. The church was built in 1853 by R.K. Penson.

The Wesleyan Chapel at Pontrobert.

The Methodist Chapel at Pontrobert.

John Hughes Chapel, Pontrobert. Built in 1800, this was the first Methodist chapel in the village. The preacher and hymn writer, John Hughes lived and died here and is buried in the nearby graveyard. He was the spiritual mentor of Ann Griffiths.

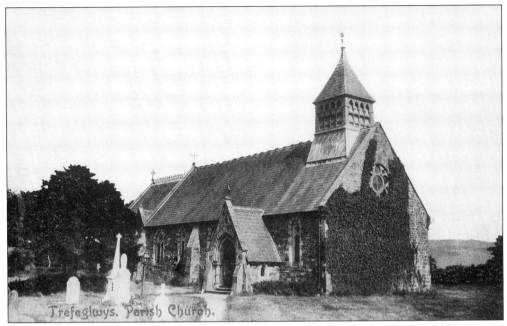

St Michael's Church, Trefegwlys. This church was substantially rebuilt in 1864-1865.

St Cynon's Church, Tregynon. There has been a church on this site since the eleventh century, but today's building dates back to the eighteenth and nineteenth centuries. The church contains several monuments relating to the Blayney family of Gregynog.

Eight

Castles, manors
and country houses

Powis Castle near Welshpool, c. 1960. In Welsh the castle is called 'Y Castell Coch' - the Red
Castle, a most relevant name as the present castle was built, largely of red sandstone, during the
thirteenth century.

Powis Castle, near Welshpool, c. 1905. During the Middle Ages this was the residence of the princes of Powys. In 1547 the castle was bought by Sir Edward Herbert and he and his successors started a long process of changes and restoration of the castle.

Powis Castle. Since 1965 the care of the castle has been in the hands of the National Trust who have carried out necessary conservation and repair work, created the Clive Museum and developed visitor facilities such as tea rooms and a shop.

Powis Castle, as seen from the main garden gate, *c*. 1960. The grounds, landscaped through the centuries, include beautiful flowers, sculptured hedges and fine pieces of stonework.

Montgomery Castle, *c.* 1905. Montgomery was of great military importance protecting the only effective way into mid-Wales. The first Norman castle, a motte and bailey earthwork, was built by Roger de Montgomery at Hendomen. The second castle was built two miles away on the present site between 1223 and 1227 by Henry III.

Montgomery Castle, *c.* 1905. During the Civil Wars the castle was surrendered to the Parliamentarian army by the owner, Edward, Lord Herbert. The castle was subsequently besieged by the Royalists leading to the Battle of Montgomery which took place on Wednesday, 18 September 1644. The Royalists lost and as a consequence mid-Wales was lost for the King. In 1649 the castle was demolished.

Leighton Hall, near Welshpool, *c.* 1905. This neo-Gothic hall, together with a model estate, was built by John Naylor in the middle of the nineteenth century. Much of the interior of the hall was built to designs by A.W.N. Pugin and resembles the Houses of Parliament to such a degree that the hall has been used in several television productions.

Llanerchydol Hall, near Welshpool, *c.* 1905. Although parts of the building may date back to the 1700s, most of the house is from the following century.

Gregynog Hall, near Newtown, *c*. 1880. The first mention of this hall dates from the twelfth century. From the fifteenth century it was the home of the Blayney family. In 1795 it passed to the Hanbury Tracy family.

Gregynog Hall, *c*. 1880. The hall was rebuilt in the nineteenth century in a mock-Jacobean style. After having changed hands several times the hall was finally sold by the first Lord Davies to his two sisters, Miss Gwendoline and Miss Margaret Davies in 1920. They were all the grandchildren of the coal magnate, David Davies of Llandinam.

Gregynog Hall, seen from the south-west, *c*. 1905. The Davies sisters developed the hall into a centre for art. They collected impressionist and post-impressionist paintings, gave musical concerts and recitals of poetry, and started the Gregynog Press - a publishing company of fine books using traditional methods. Today the hall is run by the University of Wales.

Aberhafesp Hall, near Newtown, *c*. 1905. This brick mansion dates from the late seventeenth century. Today, it has been divided into four dwellings. Reputedly, the house has a ghost: a lady in white who walks from the nearby church to the east door of the hall.

Glansevern, Berriew, near Welshpool. The house was built for Sir Arthur Davies Owen by Joseph Bromfield between *c.* 1801 and 1807. It was designed in the severe Greek revival style of the early nineteenth century.

Glanhafren, Newtown, *c*. 1905.

Caerhowel, Newtown, *c*. 1905. This mansion was built by Thomas Penson in 1858 as the residence of Lt-Col Pryce-Jones MP.

Rhiewport, Berriew, near Welshpool. This large house was built about 1815.

The south side of Maesmawr Hall, near Caersws, *c*. 1905. Originally an Elizabethan mansion, it was extensively restored and rebuilt in the eighteenth and nineteenth centuries. Today, it is a hotel.

Plas Dinam near Llandinam, *c.* 1905. Built in 1873-1874 by W.E. Nesfield, it is the home of the David Davies family.

Cyfronydd, near Welshpool, *c.* 1880. This mansion was built around 1865 as the home of the Pryce family. Today, it is a school.

OWAIN GLYNDWR
OLD PARLIAMENT HOUSE (1402).
MACHYNLLETH

Owain Glyn Dŵr's 'Old Parliament House', Machynlleth. In 1400 Owain Glyn Dŵr became the leader of a last great rising of the Welsh, against King Henry IV of England. In 1402 and 1404 Glyn Dŵr held Welsh parliaments in Machynlleth and in 1404 he was proclaimed Prince of Wales in the town. He was finally defeated by the English Prince of Wales (later Henry V), in 1410 and is believed to have died some years later c. 1415.

OWAIN GLYNDWR OLD PARLIAMENT HOUSE (1402). MACHYNLLETH

Owain Glyn Dŵr's Old Parliament House, Machynlleth. Although tradition has connected the site of this building with the Welsh parliaments held by Owain Glyn Dŵr, the house itself dates from the sixteenth century. It is very well preserved.

Owain Glyn Dŵr's Old Parliament House, Machynlleth showing the new adjoining building of the Owain Glyndwr Institute, which was built in 1911 by Lord Davies of Llandinam.

Plas Machynlleth, Machynlleth. The construction of the house stretches over two centuries; some of the building dates back to the seventeenth century, while the front was built in 1853. During the nineteenth and twentieth centuries the house was owned by the Londonderry family and many famous people visited the place including King Edward VII and Queen Alexandra, King George V and Queen Mary and Lord Randolph Churchill. In 1947 the house was given to the town.

Dolerw, Newtown, c. 1905. This house was built for Sir Pryce Pryce-Jones in 1867. Today it is St Mary and St Benedict's School.

Vaynor Park, Berriew, near Welshpool. The present building stands on the site of a medieval house. It dates back to the middle of the seventeenth century and may have been built for George Devereux, the High Sheriff at the time. It is one of only four such big brick houses of its period in the county. Since the eighteenth century, it has been in the possession of the Corbet-Winder family.

Maes Mawr Hall, Meifod, near Welshpool, c. 1905. The hall was built by a Royalist member of the Lloyd family of Trawscoed near Guilsfield. During the Commonwealth years he was in exile in Holland and when he returned following the Restoration of Charles II he was inspired by the Dutch architecture he had seen during his exile. Built from 1689 to 1692, the hall is supposedly a recreation of the Dutch style.

Trelydan Hall, Guilsfield, near Welshpool. The earliest parts date to the sixteenth century but most of the impressive black and white building is of later origin.

Trelydan Hall, Guilsfield, near Welshpool, c. 1880.

South-east frontage of Garth Hall, Guilsfield, near Welshpool, 1946. In 1809 Richard Mytton, reverend and chaplain to the Governor General of India, commissioned J.C. Loudon to build a hall on the family estate. The result was a mixture of St George's Chapel at Windsor, Ely Cathedral, Brighton Pavilion and Strawberry Hill constructed for the exorbitant price of £100,000. This bankrupted the owner and by 1939 the house stood empty. After the Second World War it was sadly demolished.

Llwyn, near Llanfyllin, *c.* 1905. A fine Georgian building, construction of the house began in 1710.

The north side of Newtown Hall, Newtown. This was the home of the Pryce family from the early fifteenth century. The hall was changed significantly in the nineteenth century and in 1965 it was demolished to make way for a new town hall.

The front entrance of Newtown Hall, Newtown. When one of the owners, the 5th Baronet, Sir John Pryce (b. 1761), married for the third time, his new wife insisted that he removed the embalmed bodies of his two previous wives from the bedroom where he had kept them since their deaths!

Lymore Hall, near Montgomery, *c.* 1900. After the demolition of Black Hall and Montgomery Castle during the Civil War this half-timbered house was built in 1675 by Edward, 3rd Lord Herbert of Chirbury.

Lymore Hall, near Montgomery. After the Herberts moved their residence to Powis Castle near Welshpool, the hall was rarely used. The last overnight guests stayed in 1886 although there were royal visitors at the beginning of the twentieth century.

Lymore Hall, near Montgomery, c. 1880. In 1927 the building was found to be structurally unsound by the Royal Commission and it was demolished in the 1930s. Some of the interior details have been moved to, and used, in other buildings.